Undivided Attention

Undivided Attention

Poems by

Milton J. Bates

© 2025 Milton J. Bates. All rights reserved.
This material may not be reproduced in any form, published,
reprinted, recorded, performed, broadcast,
rewritten, or redistributed without
the explicit permission of Milton J. Bates.
All such actions are strictly prohibited by law.

Cover design by Shay Culligan
Cover image by Milton J. Bates
Author photo by Elizabeth J. Bates

ISBN: 978-1-63980-683-6
Library of Congress Control Number: 2025933263

Kelsay Books
502 South 1040 East, A-119
American Fork, Utah 84003
Kelsaybooks.com

for Zoe and Sam

Acknowledgments

This collection includes poems that first appeared, some in slightly different form, in the following publications:

Always on Fire chapbook: "Listening to September"
Awake in the World anthology, volume 2: "Coming of Age on the Escanaba"
California Quarterly: "Fire Season"
Cloudbank: "Anywhere but Home," "To a Tiny Flycatcher"
Consequence: "Man Down" (under title "Casualty")
Crosswinds: "Tucking In"
Encore: Prize Poems 2014 and 2015 (NFSPS anthologies): "Chinese Folk Song Performed on Oldest Playable Flute," "Transmigration"
Great Lakes Review: "Mushroom Hunters," "You Are Here"
Home anthology (Outrider Press): "Living Room"
Lullabies and Confessions anthology: "Zoe Dances"
Maine Review: "Born to Be Wild"
Peninsula Poets: "Chosen," "Golden," "The Picture Above Our Bed," "Shifting Gears"
Ponder Review: "My First Deer"
Proud to Be: Writing by American Warriors anthology, volume 12: "The Green Trunk"
Running with Water anthology: "Against All Odds"
SPLASH! (Haunted Waters Press online): "Pact"
Stoneboat: "Guy walks into a bar"
Superior Voyage anthology: "Missing Sisters Found Safe"
Wallace Stevens Journal: "A Pretext for Poetry"
Walloon Writers Review: "First Fall," "Preserves," "Salamander Nights," selected "Soundbites"

Contents

I. Here

You Are Here	15
Our Jacobsville Foundation	16
Spring Soundbites	17
Missing Sisters Found Safe	18
April	20
Salamander Nights	21
Symbiosis	22
Storm Warning	23
Outage	24
Coming of Age on the Escanaba	25
Summer Soundbites	27
Getting Air	28
Born to Be Wild	29
Fungi	30
Big Cat	31
Grace	32
Preserves	33
Fall Soundbites	34
Listening to September	35
Harvest Supermoon over Superior	36
First Fall	37
Tucking In	38
Fire Season	39
Second Coming	40
My First Deer	41
Winter Soundbites	43
Shifting Gears	44
The Persistence of Tinsel	45
Making the Most of It	46
Against All Odds	47
Anywhere but Home	48

II. Briefings

Side View	51
Man Down	52
All but One	53
On Learning, at 79, My Life Expectancy Was 72	54

III. What Wings Are For

Chinese Folk Song Performed on Oldest Playable Flute	57
View from the Back Row	58
Skagit Valley Snow Geese	59
Tomales Bay Ravens	60
Learning How to Be a Bird	61
Merganser Hen Meets Sam	62
Sheltering in Place	63
Opus Steps Up	64
To a Tiny Flycatcher	65
John Muir's Dipper	66
Transmigration	68
Chosen	69
Redirection	71

IV. Pretexts

A Pretext for Poetry	75
Encysted	76
Mona Lisa Responds to Latest Assault	77
Guy walks into a bar	78
23 and Me	79
Living Room	81

Haunted	82
Mushroom Hunters	83
Couch Diving	84
The Revenant	85
The Green Trunk	87
My Grandfather's Kodak	88
The Handoff	89
Golden	90
Zoe Dances	91
The Picture Above Our Bed	92
The Good Ship *Point Reyes*	93
Pact	94
My eyes, those two candles	95

I. Here

You Are Here

Yes and no.

i. Yes

A red dot marks the spot
where two black lines converge.
You've been hiking one, will
turn and hike the other.

It's a geometry
of the gods, who can see
where your story's going,
how it begins and ends.

ii. No

The red dot is nothing
like the dirt beneath your
boots. The black lines level
the sweaty uphill climb.

The color is all wrong.
Where are sound, feel, smell?
The *here* on the trail sign
is not the here you know.

Our Jacobsville Foundation

Lake Superior licks the sandstone bluff
downhill from our house. Uphill, our road
meanders along an older lakeshore.
So it goes, terrace above terrace, as you
climb hills once high as the Himalayas.

A billion years ago, those dying mountains
repaired a rift in Earth's crust. Weather wore
them down to nubs, flushing grains of iron-rich
rock into the breach. The sediment turned
rust-red except where leaching left it white.
We've built red cities with blocks of that
sandstone. It filters the water we drink.

Follow an ancient shoreline where tentacles
of pine and hemlock cling to outcrops,
where moss and lichen flourish on stone
laid down when life was still in embryo.
It's a good place to walk, especially when
you need to heal a rift, find a foothold,
or put your little life in perspective.

Spring Soundbites

The ice honeycombs
and sinks in the lake, fizzing
like freshly poured Coke.

Cranes in the cornfield
bugle a welcome to those
still circling above.

Pinecones crunch when stepped
on, their seeds released last fall
to fatten squirrels.

An outboard cranks, coughs,
and catches, its hum trailing
the boat like a wake.

Nuthatches *yank-yank*
on their kazoos as they graze
insects from tree trunks.

One peeper starts up.
Another chimes in. Soon all
are jingling their bells.

Soft tattoo of rain
on roof, then a metallic
tinkling in downspouts.

Missing Sisters Found Safe

April 24, 2015

The sisters were sure it was a bear,
emerging hungry from its den in April.
It must have smelled the Girl Scout cookies
and Cheetos. They locked the doors of their
Ford Explorer and tried to sleep.
                                     At daybreak
on Day Thirteen, the landscape still looked nothing
like the places they called home, Nebraska
and Oklahoma. Deep woods and deeper snow,
an unplowed two-track to nowhere. But it
was all nowhere, wasn't it, in this part
of Michigan?
                   Thank God for their bible,
the Cheetos, those eight boxes of cookies.
New this year were Toffee-tastic and Rah-Rah
Raisins. Holding their breakfast ration like
communion wafers, they gave thanks and chewed
them slowly, savoring the sugar. Maybe
next year the GSA would issue cookies
in their honor, call them—what? Leslie Lees?
Assuming they survived, Lee and Leslie
would vouch for their virtue in the field, claim
they were the peer of army MREs
and NASA food pouches, not that they'd
ever tasted either.

                    Just then they heard
a distant roar. The bear was back, or so
they thought, until a chopper cleared the treetops.
Well, it was about time. They stepped out
to wave like those people on the TV news,
stranded on their roof when a levee failed.
Now they would have to explain how they'd
missed the turn to Mackinaw City.
Which got them both to thinking: instead of
Leslie Lees, how about Mackinaw-roons?

April

dares us to see ourselves
in the marsh releasing
its lifeblood to a creek.

Cattail stems support a pane
of ice that once glazed water.
The glass is old and etched.

It obscures what lies
below: muck and matted reeds,
the squalor of starting over.

Salamander Nights

What was all the fuss about,
he wondered, that drizzly
April night in Presque Isle Park.

So much commotion and noise,
so many restless bodies
on the wide asphalt river.

Though stiff from cold and blinded
by flashlights, he stayed on course
over pavement and snow crust

to the party at the bog. How
they would admire his sky-blue
spots, his midnight-colored skin.

Symbiosis

She's a red fox, a red so muted
she's barely visible at dusk
and dawn, when she leaves her kits
under a neighbor's shed to hunt

and forage. Before sunrise one
spring morning, I placed a mousetrap
complete with mouse outside my door,
to be emptied later in the woods.

Later, it was gone. One day passed.
Another. On the third day,
it reappeared where I'd left it,
minus the mouse. I understood

the vixen's proposition: *Leave me
a full trap, and I'll return it
for a refill.* Can you trust
a creature known for its cunning,

no contract or handshake? Perhaps
you can, when both sides benefit.
She'd get a quick snack for her pups
and save me a trip to the woods.

Rather than risk my mousetrap, though,
I tweaked our arrangement slightly.
She still finds mice outside my door,
but they're no longer served on trap.

Storm Warning

First, the slightest commotion
of aspen leaves, as though they
repeat a rumor more felt
than heard, more sensed than felt.

Then the ferns behave like plants
submerged, swirling in eddies,
lifting with the rising tide,
flattening in the backwash.

Slower to respond, a yellow
birch raises and lowers its
ponderous limbs like a great
bird priming its wings for flight.

Tallest of our trees, a white spruce
pokes its needle into the eye
of the wind and feels its fury,
pummeled north to south, east to west.

See that spindrift torn from crest
or wave? Let it not be us.
Rather, that seagull rowing hard
upwind so as to stay in place.

Outage

We could picture the tree collapsing
on a power line, could feel the great ball
of darkness rolling up the road to our house.
The wind had warned us. We were prepared
with jugs of filtered water, wood stacked
beside the woodstove, cell phone batteries
charged. We had headlamps and candles, books
to read by their light. We could wait it out.

Or could we? The wind grew louder, splashed
windows with wet snow. Trees thrashed about
like dervishes, lit up by lightning.
We read the same sentence over and over
in our books, unable to concentrate.

When power resumed with an audible
jolt, blinding light, and numbers blinking
on digital clocks, we shrugged as if
to say *Well, wasn't that fun? No major
inconvenience.* We didn't mention,
and never will, how it stirred ancestral
memories of icy caves, smoking torches,
shadows writhing on walls and ceiling.

Coming of Age on the Escanaba

Never had life so gripped the boy
as on that June evening, following
his father through a dew-drenched
meadow to the river. Mayflies swarmed
the sky, a blizzard of Brown Drakes
caught up in courtship dance.
Some brushed his cheeks like snowflakes;
others clung to his clothes and fly rod.

Stepping into the slick black water,
he felt the chill through his waders
and braced against the downstream push.
He could see no nymphs, but knew
they were there, erupting from
the streambed around his boots.
They would kick to the surface, unfold
their wings, and join the aerial ball.

His father pointed with his rod
toward dimples where trout sucked down
the spinners spent from mating.
Awkwardly, as though walking on
the moon, he stalked a nearby swirl
and stripped out line. He cast and mended,
cast and mended and retrieved,
quickening the tuft of hair and hackle.

He couldn't tell just when the motion
became unconscious, when it merged
with the current that swept from sand
and gravel to water, from water to air
and back again, back to the river
where browns and brookies pastured,
where the boy could feel, as never before,
the surge of life and the tug of death.

Summer Soundbites

Loons channel the lake's
changing moods with mournful wail
and manic laughter.

Towel-wrapped and shod
in flip-flops, a girl slap-slaps
down boardwalk to beach.

Lawn mowers make more
noise, but the sprinkler's *pst! pst!*
gets your attention.

Cruising for flesh to
tickle and bite, mosquitoes
whine like dental drills.

At nightfall crickets
relieve cicadas, chopping
their buzz into chirps.

On the Fourth, what else?
A symphony of booms, pops,
whistles, and splatters.

An open window
inhales cool air and darkness,
exhales soft voices.

Getting Air

*The more we learn about "thin air,"
the more substantial it becomes.*
—Lyall Watson

A lake falls from the sky, shapeless
and shoreless. It rides the trade winds
over oceans, mountains, deserts,
and cities, ingesting red dust
from Utah, sand from the Sahara,
ash from burning forests, effusions
of smokestacks and feedlots, a newborn's
first breath, an old man's last gasp.

It chases its tail in tornadoes
and waterspouts, leaps onto
thermals cooked up by the sun.
From helix to helix it shifts,
but mostly descends, growing thick
with spores and pollen, bacteria
and viruses, algae and fungi.

Condensing at last in a bowl
of landlocked water, it accepts
that shoreline as its own. Its fish,
plants, and plankton feed on health
and harm from half a world away.

On gusty afternoons wind surfers
tack to gather speed, then go for
a forward loop, soaring, spinning,
stoked to be getting air. On misty
mornings the lake exhales a cloud
that rises shapeless and shoreless
toward the sky, looking for a lift.

Born to Be Wild

We rarely saw Mrs. Saari after
she broke her hip. Mending kept her indoors
most of a Michigan winter. When she
reappeared in spring, she was steering
a walker with wheels and handbrakes down
her driveway. The wheels chattered unsteadily
on gravel, but she didn't dare try them
on the highway that bordered her front yard.

Things got worse that summer, when the county
replaced the old bridge over Compeau Creek.
Concrete barriers arrived to shunt traffic
onto a makeshift bridge. Then a crane
with wrecking ball chugged into place beside
Mrs. Saari's mailbox. Now her home
looked like a one-house city under siege.

You won't believe this, my wife said one
morning, looking out our front window.
I thought she meant the wrecking ball at first,
lit by a sunrise that seemed to welcome
the new planet to our solar system.
Then beneath the ball I saw a tiny
figure on the stretch of pavement closed to cars.

Mrs. Saari gripped the handlebars
and leaned into her machine as though taking
a headwind full in the face. Ten yards north
and turn, ten yards south and turn. She wasn't
going far, but she was going fast.

Fungi

They are the ultimate
networkers, partnering
with tree roots to grow
great forests, with algae
to tag tree trunks
with lichen graffiti.

Shy of sunlight, they work
beneath the surface,
weaving webs intricate
as any spun by spider.

They seem to weave themselves,
as though their filaments
were thoughts of a mind
that thinks its way through
soil, rock, plants, animals.

We're not truly lifeless,
you and I, till fungi
find nothing more
to salvage from our remains.

Big Cat

A women's group broke the news on Facebook.
People had seen *some sort of big cat*
at a scenic overlook near town. No
eyewitnesses stepped forward, yet details
multiplied on the website like germs
in a petri dish: the cat had a long tail;
officers from Natural Resources
escorted visitors back to their cars.

The postings seemed plausible. For years,
trail cams had captured ghostly images
of cougars drifting from the Dakotas
into our part of Upper Michigan.
Would a big cat risk a tourist magnet
like Sugarloaf Mountain? Locals doubted it,
but a few went to see for themselves.

Arriving at the summit unscathed, they
took in the familiar spectacle of woods
dropping down to lake, lake lapping against
horizon. Try as they might to give
such beauty its due, the climbers were
distracted by an unfamiliar prickle
at nape of neck. What might be stalking
them, they wondered, in this wild, wild place?

Grace

Seek and you shall find, the gospels say,
though he wasn't seeking when he found it,
just walking in the woods. The spectral shape
appeared and disappeared among the ferns—
a deer unlike any he'd seen before,
white as the unicorn in old tapestries.

He'd come to the woods expecting nothing,
no burning bush or speaking cloud. Surely
the deer would startle at his approach?
But no; it browsed unperturbed as it crossed
a clearing and paused on the other side
to fix him with pale pink eyes. Then it was
gone, its whiteness blotted by green balsams.

When he was young and ripe for revelation,
he'd found nothing he sought. Had he been
looking in the wrong places? Or had
the seeking itself kept him from finding?
He sat what seemed a lifetime in his car,
key in hand, before he could start the engine.

Preserves

I spill a pint of thimbleberries
onto a cookie sheet, then spread
them out to winnow bits of leaf,
the occasional insect or grub.

How many there are, how much alike.
Yet each was chosen from those less ripe
on its nodding stem, each red gem
slipped carefully from its green bezel.

Is this the one I climbed a bank
to harvest? Is that the one
a mosquito made me pay for?

Sugared and simmered in a saucepan,
the berries will shed their shape
and separateness, dissolve into
the anonymity of jam.

I write these words to preserve
not the fruit itself but the picking,
to keep its sweet and tart from getting
lost, like so many sensations,
in the jampot of memory.

Fall Soundbites

The arthritic old
house shifts and creaks, adjusting
to change of season.

Rain freezes on trees,
turning branches to wind chimes
that click and rattle.

A grouse explodes from
aspen cover, desperate
to be somewhere else.

Sandstone caves resound
with guttural *whumps* when storms
drive big lake swells in.

Behind the woodpile
dry leaves swirl up and rattle,
poised as though to strike.

Canning jars form up
for inspection by the stove,
popping as they cool.

Woodstove warmth begins
with the cellophane crackle
of twigs igniting.

Listening to September

Our noisy summer guests have slipped away
without so much as a goodbye,
leaving local residents to wonder
whether the place is really theirs again.

A chickadee tries out a riff we haven't heard
since spring, then stops to listen. What it hears,
we hear too: a peeper's high-pitched note,
sounding at intervals day and night.

In May that soloist was one of many
in a grand chorale. A gray tree frog chimes in
now and then, squeezing from the bagpipe
at its throat a deeper, reedy trill. Are these
the diehards, not quite ready to call it
a season? Or youngsters trying out
for parts in next summer's ensemble?

Soon the frost will slow their pulses too,
and mute their music. They will burrow
under leaves and listen like the rest of us
for the chickadee's breezy wakeup call.

Harvest Supermoon over Superior

Neither smith nor smithy can
be seen, yet a ball of fiery
metal lifts above the horizon.

At first, its molten redness seeps
to either side, deflected
by breath of lake and wisp of cloud.

Higher up, the metal cools,
contracts to minted coin, lights
a silver path on the water.

The smith can't linger to admire
his work. By dawn tomorrow
he must forge a hotter, brighter sphere.

First Fall

Soon the maple leaves will crash
and burn, their red and orange flames
lighting up rain-blackened roads.
The trees will turn to skeletons.

But first the white pines must shed
their annual crop of yellow
needles. Five-strawed whisks carpet
our yard, brightening dead stalks
of bee balm and black-eyed Susan.

Some tick against the window
coming down, then link with others
on our deck to spell out cryptic
messages in Viking runes.

Tell us your secret, great pines.
How can you spend all that gold,
yet remain so green and glossy?

Tucking In

As temperatures drop and days
lose daylight, we retreat from deck
and porch to woodstove, where soon
we'll light the first fire of fall.

The animals draw inward too,
some to their own nests, some to ours.
Red squirrels take refuge under
the rafters in our garage.

Mice scavenge the sunflower seed
scattered beneath our bird feeder.
We find caches in a slipper,
a drawer, the foot of our bed.

Even the plants are closing in.
See that sugar maple blazing
like a torch outside our window?
Its roots creep up a basement drain.

How provident these creatures are.
But our boundaries get firmer
as the air gets colder. We are
tucking in and buttoning up,

contracting to our inmost selves
like the seeds we're saving for spring.

Fire Season

Our granddaughter's face looms larger
as she leans into her computer screen
two thousand miles away. Summer heat
still lingers in Sonoma, plumping grapes
and keeping people close to air conditioners.
We sit close to our woodstove in Michigan,
ready to light the first fire of October.

Zoe joins us by laptop, placed on a stool
between us. She watches the flames leap
from newspaper to cedar kindling,
then caress the smaller splits of maple.

We watch the fire reflected in her eyes,
not our fire only, but fire as children
know it where she lives, the word whispered
or spelled out between parents packing
a suitcase for evacuation. Those days,
the sun is an ember in ashen sky.

What brings up the blood in Zoe's face?
Is she relieved to see nightmare contained
in cast iron? Outside, a hard frost
whitens our world. Indoors, we inhale
sweet spice of cedar and bask, all three
of us, in the afterglow of summer.

Second Coming

When aspen catkins burst with seed
this spring, tiny cotton clouds took
to the air, rising and falling,
swirling in eddies till sieved by
window screens or swept into drifts.

Did any of those seeds find
receptive soil? One is enough
to start a forest—not aspens
plural but aspen as organic
whole, spreading underground until,
like Pando in Utah, its roots
infiltrate a hundred acres.

If any tree could get religion,
surely it would be the quaking
aspen, its leaves a-shimmer
with light, responsive to subtlest
visitations of spirit.

Jesus will come in judgment, some
believe, when aspens cease to quake.
The trees rehearse their part each fall,
dropping their gold to listen,
motionless, for the trumpet blast
that announces the Rapture.

My First Deer

> *He pulled trigger and Sam Fathers marked his face with the hot blood which he had spilled and he ceased to be a child and became a hunter and a man.*
> —William Faulkner, "The Old People"

First Deer, says the caption beneath the photo.
The rest is about the boy of thirteen,
maybe fourteen, who steers the antlered head
into the lens, its tongue spilling from the side

of its muzzle. The camera's flash has gouged
the pupils from its eyes, turned them to glass.
It's a generic shot, a seasonal staple
of small-town newspapers. Another kid,

another carcass. This boy's buck is like
the one I might have killed when I was
his age. I'd hardly slept the night before,
awake for every *whoosh* of the propane

heater kicking in, the riot of mice
above the ceiling, the death-rattle snoring
of the grizzled veterans. At sunrise
I was on my stand, my .30-30 ready.

I pictured my first deer gliding across
the creek and into range. It would present
its profile and await the consummation
of a bullet. My father would slit its throat

like the old hunter in Faulkner's story.
When he smeared my face with blood, I'd become
a man. That's how it was supposed to happen,
that easy, provided my deer chose the trail

I watched. Which of course it didn't, not that fall
or any that followed, so I had to muddle
through to manhood without the sacrament.
It was a messier way, though bloodless.

Yet I hope that first deer in the photo gives
the boy as much in death as mine gave me
in life, year after year until it fell
to winter, wolves, or another hunter.

Winter Soundbites

Wind plays a somber
solo on double bass, bare
branch rubbing bare branch.

Flushed from roadside feast
by passing cars, ravens croak
their disappointment.

Skis whisper and glide,
shushing the angry hornet
drone of snowmobiles.

Frost cracks its bullwhip
in the woods, splitting the skin
of smooth-barked maples.

You can tell it's cold
when snow squeaks underfoot like
an old farmhouse floor.

Released long after
those from other trees, oak leaves
skitter on snow crust.

Ice is booming on
the lake tonight, a drumroll
for the Northern Lights.

Shifting Gears

They recommended *baby steps,* at first,
to winter visitors who needed coaching
when they ventured onto icy surfaces.

The phrase sufficed for older folks, but those
closer to babyhood merely covered
less ground before they went down flailing.

So with lowered voices they told the youngsters
to walk *like old people.* Now the group
arrived intact at restaurants and shops.

After guests departed and winter gave
way to spring, their flat-footed shuffle
evolved into something like a step.

By summer it had lengthened to a stride.
How good it felt to be moving smartly!
When fall glazed sidewalks with freezing rain,

no one had to tell the locals how
to walk. Some downshifted to baby steps;
others inched along like old people.

The Persistence of Tinsel

When we drape our Christmas tree
in tinsel, always the final touch,
it transforms that backwoods girl
into a Roaring Twenties flapper.

The silver fringe on her dress
shimmies in the slightest breeze,
multiplying by a million
the light of electric bulbs.

Though dazzled by her bravura,
we pay a price. Approach too close,
and we come away wearing silver.
For weeks we'll mine it from sweaters,

coats, carpets, blankets, whatever
she took a fancy to. Is her
attire worth all the trouble?
Maybe not. Yet we'll remember

her and smile on a sultry day
in August when, like a magician,
I pluck from behind your ear
a silvery strand of December.

Making the Most of It

Before cooking became an art,
the province of celebrity chefs,
it was a way to pre-digest
our food, easing the work of stomach
enzymes and gut bacteria.

Pity the poor snowshoe hare,
having to subsist in winter
on twigs and bark. Fireless, it must
eat its own waste, pass it through
the mill again to salvage protein
and vitamins from the roughage.

In November, when patches
of snow mottled the brown landscape,
snowshoes were likewise calicoes.

Slogging through January snow
today, you follow a trail
of pellets and exclamation
points till you find a snowshoe
huddled beneath a balsam.
Its button eyes and black-tipped ears
are the only morsels winter
hasn't managed to consume.

Against All Odds

In a warm office somewhere overseas,
a computer feeds dogs and mushers
into an algorithm that chooses
the odds-on favorite to win the race.

But don't tell the dogs at the starting line,
restrained by handlers in white bibs.
They yip and whine, churning the snow
in place, frantic to be on their way.

Don't tell the musher, who jogs a few yards
at send-off, then steps onto the footboards.
He waves to the crowd that lines the street,
ringing cowbells to speed him on his way.

Don't tell the people whose cheers rise
like balloons toward the moon. Knowing
nothing of the odds, they don't doubt
that this sled, too, could finish first.

And please don't tell the two-year-old perched
on her father's shoulders. She lifts a mittened
hand to the passing blur of dogs and musher,
bidding them goodbye, wishing them good luck.

Anywhere but Home

Suppose Boccaccio had followed his
Florentine storytellers when they left
their refuge from the plague. Suppose that Poe's
Prince Prospero and his court had escaped
the Red Death, that Camus' Doctor Rieux
had chronicled life in reopened Oran.

How would those survivors have behaved
in a sequel? Would they have sought revenge
on the pathogen that kept them in villa,
abbey, and gated city with money
to spend but little to spend it on?

We spend freely, those of us who can,
on post-pandemic travel. Desperate
to be anywhere but home, we book flights,
cruises, vacation rentals. We push wild-eyed
through crowds at Yellowstone and Yosemite,
frantic to claim our share before it's too late,
before it's all gone, before we too are gone.

And then? Boccaccio can't help us there,
nor can Poe or Camus. But here is what
they might advise: Go home. Unlock the door
and enter. Set down your bags. Breathe deeply.
If living well is the best revenge, you'll
find no better place to settle that score.

II. Briefings

Side View

Except for splashes
of insect on the windshield,
the view ahead
looks clear and promising.

Passing a church
with open door, I check
my side view mirror
as men in black trundle
a box to the curb.

A warning on the mirror
says objects like these
are closer than they appear.

Man Down

for B. H., 1981–2021

When our nation finally
withdrew from the twenty-year
war we couldn't win, those
who'd fought in Afghanistan
had plenty to say if asked
whether they felt their service
had been worth it.
                Where we live
on Lake Superior, one of them
said nothing, just launched his kayak
as he often did when he needed
to be alone.
           Searchers found
the boat overturned offshore.
They found the body eighteen
days later, weighted down
in death as he was in life.

All but One

*How many dead people
are in that cemetery?*
my mother would ask
when we drove past one
of those gardens of stone.

All of them! she'd say
after a pause, laughing
as much at our groans
as at the old joke.

Passing a cemetery
today, I remember
that laugh and am happy
to find her still alive
after so many years,
among so many dead.

On Learning, at 79, My Life Expectancy Was 72

It takes me longer
than most people

to read a book,
eat a meal, or drive
from here to there;

so of course
I'm taking longer
to live my life.

III. What Wings Are For

Chinese Folk Song Performed on Oldest
Playable Flute

It was all about air, how it passes
over mortal things. When the bone was
still fleshed and fledged, it made a slight
creaking sound as the great bird flew
over mountains. It lay mute and folded
as the bird stilt-walked the marshes
or clamored with the other red-crowns,
their slender bills pointing skyward
like reeds along the Yellow River.

The bone survived the bird. A man
of Jiahu drilled seven holes for air to come
and go as his lips and fingers pleased.
Even then the bone sang its own song,
an elegy for cranes and men, as though
it could hear the coming silence, foresee
the nine millennia of midnight.

At last a hand reached out of light
to lift the bone, clay-clotted, from its grave.
Soon it felt lips again, and fingers,
teasing air into tendrils of melody.
It half-learned and half-remembered
how Little Cabbage missed her mother,
especially in spring, when the air
was sweet with peach and almond blossoms.

View from the Back Row

One summer a robin attacked its own
reflection in our kitchen window till
we were sure it would break either glass
or beak. The bird got crazier as weeks
went by and shocks to its brain added up.

That fall our first-grade teacher, Sister
Mary Amabilis, had each of us sing
the notes she played on her pitch pipe.
When she pasted a robin sticker
on my sweater, I knew I was assigned
to the back row in our Christmas choral
program, unheard and almost unseen
behind the meadow larks and orioles.

It's enough to drive you crazy, seeing
your worst enemy in the mirror, rasping
like Tom Waits among Sinatras. Then
you remember those kids in Wisconsin,
first to choose the robin as state bird
over more gifted thrushes. May we love
in ourselves what endeared us to them,
even if only our familiar presence.

Skagit Valley Snow Geese

From a distance they look like goose
down shaken onto a field disked
for spring planting. The whiteness
spreads as dozens join them for
the night, seeking safety in numbers.

What they fear takes definite form
when an eagle wings over, then
a second and a third. The geese
take to the air as one, a cloud
of troubled thought. The eagles probe
their perimeter, wolves around
a flock of sheep, but find no stragglers.

When the eagles fly off, the goose
down settles back to earth still
salted with last year's grain, fuel
for this year's three thousand miles
to an island in the Arctic Sea.

Tomales Bay Ravens

When she rises from their nest on a snag
overlooking the bay, fluffs her vest and preens
her wing feathers, her mate understands
it's time to retrieve a morsel from their
secret cache. Beak to beak he feeds her,
then guards the eggs as she flies to a tree
nearby, far enough to stretch her wings,
close enough to keep the nest in sight.

We watch from a window, sharing a pair
of binoculars. One of us pours coffee
and hands the other a cup. Observing
our morning ritual, the birds might wonder
which sex is which, whether we also
breed and brood. Yes, we could assure them,
after our fashion. But rarely have we
witnessed parenting as harmonious
as theirs or as free of human brooding.

Learning How to Be a Bird

Preschool begins midsummer
for fledglings. By late August they're
already in high school, a time
as awkward for them as for us.

An eagle in training swoops down
to snatch a lake trout, fumbles
the fish, and has to circle back.
Young ravens try to mimic their
parents' authoritative croak,
but manage only the godawful
squawks of first-tuners on
clarinet. A nuthatch, curious
and trusting as Darwin's finches,
wonders if that cat will be its friend.

Those that survive to graduation
detect in their elders a sense
of urgency as days grow shorter
and cooler. Something is about
to happen, they don't know what,
but they itch for adventure, maybe
travel, before they settle down.
What are wings for, if not to fly?

Merganser Hen Meets Sam

She leads a dozen fluffy ducklings down Harlow Creek to Lake Superior. In a pool created by a sandbar at the mouth, she shows them how to skim the water with their bills for tiny organisms. When any stray, she circles her brood and cinches them into a tighter knot. Then she repeats her demonstration.

On one of these roundups, she notices the creature sitting in the shallows. How alien it appears—featherless and shockingly white, as though plucked. Yet also attentive, unlike a few of her own offspring. Will this chubby youngster thrive without her coaching? Maybe so. Still, it was missing out on some delectable tidbits.

Sheltering in Place

Zoom In

Descend from moon to redwood tree,
a quarter of a million miles.
From tree a final, easy glide
to the campsite where they sleep
in their tent after hot chocolate
and marshmallows toasted over
coals. They've seen stars and fireflies,
heard a barred owl's eerie solo
and the soothing spill of water.
The child stirs in her sleeping bag,
but doesn't wake as on other nights,
troubled by something she can't name.

Zoom Out

The sun climbs over the eastern
hills to light the redwood's topmost
taper. Within the wooden fence,
their stockade, water still pulses
from the fountain pump. Last night's
ashes lie cold in the firepit.

Riding the thermals high above,
a red-tailed hawk watches parents
and child retreat into a house
with breakfast, indoor plumbing,
and news of a world stalked by plague.
The redtail has no name for that
contagion, nor for the health they seek,
and sometimes find, in soaring hawks.

Opus Steps Up

Who would have thought that a flightless bird could inspire such flights of fancy? This particular penguin, a stuffed simulacrum of Berke Breathed's cartoon character, had gathered dust for decades on our bookshelf. Turns out, he was merely biding his time, awaiting his finest hour.

It arrived in 2020, when the Covid pandemic threw our son's household into disarray—both parents trying, like so many, to work from home with a restive five-year-old out of school and craving their attention.

Grandma, bless her heart, volunteered to babysit by Zoom. But there are only so many children's classics to read, only so many craft projects to supervise. That's when Opus came forward to offer his penguin perspective on the day's challenges.

California's heat and smoky air seemed less oppressive compared with Antarctic cold, and Zoe was happy to forgo her new friend's steady diet of fish. Opus made her laugh with his squeaky voice and whimsical musings. Once, he pasted a postage stamp on his bulbous nose and hid in Grandma's mailbox, hoping to travel parcel post to Sonoma.

He finally made that trip two years later, on a commercial flight. Did he live up to a seven-year-old's expectations? Our heroes always seem smaller, don't they, in real life? More like us. But if Opus lost stature in Zoe's eyes; if he became just another plush toy like those on her bed, she kept that disappointment to herself.

To a Tiny Flycatcher

You found us in the fog offshore,
trolling for lake trout, our boat
slowly unzipping the silky
surface. You arrived as though
expected, as though our party
was incomplete without you.

You troll in your own way, flying
sorties into the haze of insects
that hover just above the water.
We hold our breath when your wings
beat against the lake like a moth
at the window. Will it suck you
under this time? It never does.
You return to your roost on rod tip,
shake out your raincoat, and bob
to the pulse of the trolling spoon.

Suppose that rod were suddenly
to register the violence
of unseen life. Would it whip you
forever from our sphere? We'll find out
if a laker strikes. Meanwhile, we're
blessed to have you as companion
and figurehead, the visible
genius of a vast invisibility.

John Muir's Dipper

*Among all mountain birds, none has cheered
me so much in my lonely wanderings.*
—John Muir

Watching it dip for insects
and larvae in a mountain stream
swollen with snow and glacier melt,
you might mistake it for a shorebird.
Then it surprises you, plunging
into the torrent to walk or swim
submerged, as though water were
as much its element as air.

The dipper's aquadynamic
shape reminded Muir of
a pebble whirled in a pothole.
He admired in particular
its good cheer in desperate weather.
While most birds sulked silently
through a Yosemite snowstorm,
a dipper lifted his spirits
with intricate melody.

We saw our first dipper where Muir
saw his, in the Merced River.
Behind a waterfall nearby,
we found its hive-shaped nest, woven
of moss and grasses. Years later,
hiking up a creekside trail
in Alaska, we paused to watch
dipper parents dive repeatedly
to feed their hungry fledgling.

So wedded are the birds to their
native streams, Muir conjectured,
that a tracing of their flights would
chart the flow of Western rivers
and the ice sheets that fed them.

A map of our movements would show
how far we've strayed from our first
watershed. Yet we've always nested
near streams that sluice through valleys
or pool in lake or ocean. Sometimes
we merely dip in those waters.
Sometimes, like dippers, we dive.

Transmigration

To the jay it must have seemed as though
a thunderbolt had struck it from its perch.
It lay in snow beneath the feeder, stunned,

after other birds dispersed. So many eyes,
yet none had seen the dark comet coming
through the balsams. The chosen one resisted

briefly as the sharp-shin's talons probed its breast
and throat. Then it relaxed, its black eyes
focused on the distance like a martyr

or jihadist contemplating paradise.
It hardly felt the beak that rummaged
through its down and ripped its belly open.

Shifting its grip, the hawk hauled out
smoking viscera, tugging as a robin
tugs at earthworms. It dipped repeatedly

for meat, for heat, for fluid in a frozen world.
Bit by bit one life became another.
What lifted off and flew away was neither

hawk nor jay but both, a mythic bird.
A plaque of feathers marks the place of rapture,
sky-blue with dabs of black and white.

Chosen

Can you choose your totem, or does it choose
you? In the Cascades that spring, mine chose me
as surely as my parents chose my name.

The sun had cleared the snow from a campsite
on Jakey Lake, but wouldn't linger long.
I shrugged off my backpack, jointed up

a fishing rod, and hustled to a pool
of twilight bordered by snow and jack pines.
A fallen tree served as dock, inclining

toward deep water. Again and again
I cast, my line catching light like spider
filament. That's all it caught, or so

I thought, until I felt the bird alight,
its Brancusi form familiar on my boot:
a red-breasted nuthatch. With tentative

beak it tapped first the rivet on a lace
hook. No insect eggs or grubs detained
it there, so up my leg it climbed, solving

with its toes the mystery of blue
denim bark. My jacket may have felt less
peculiar underfoot, its wool like moss

or lichens. *Where to next?* the climber
seemed to ask when perched at last on my
shoulder. I could see my face reflected

in the miniscule black bead of its eye.
Then, answering its own question, it flew
off in search of more productive trees.

I turned back toward camp, my trout pool drowned
in darkness. Can you feel at once diminished
and exalted—no bigger than a bird's eye,

yet larger for that eye's election?
I'd caught what I needed there, and wished
my totem equal luck in foraging.

Redirection

September 26, 2022

The blue-shirted crew in NASA's mission
control room leap to their feet and cheer,
then trade high fives when their spaceship DART
(for Double Asteroid Redirection Test)
                       hits the bullseye.

In that borough of heaven reserved
for dinosaurs, the larger thunder lizards
remember the day an asteroid turned
their tropical world to deadly winter
                       and sigh *if only*.

The pterosaurs perished too, but not
all birds. Observing the NASA team,
they feel a surge of pride almost parental,
amazed how quickly those wingless bipeds
                       have mastered flight.

Proud of us, whose inner space is no less
perilous than outer? The inner swarms
with rage for war, with lust to ravage Earth.
Redirect those urges, and we may survive—
                       but only if.

IV. Pretexts

A Pretext for Poetry

The faintness and strangeness of the sound made on me one of those impressions which one so often seizes as pretexts for poetry.
—Wallace Stevens

Elsewhere, it might have been a man treading
shards of glass in the alley behind
a bar or a woman in her kitchen,
crushing croutons with a rolling pin.

Here on Westerly Terrace in Hartford,
it is a cat crossing a lawn encrusted
with snow that had melted and re-frozen,
each blade of grass a minor stalagmite.

What does it hunt on this moonlit night
in November? Most birds have gone south,
chipmunks dream of summer in their burrows,
and the cat is belled by what it walks on.

This may be no ordinary cat
stalking ordinary prey. It may be
Bastet, daughter of Ra and Isis, come
from her temple on the Nile to rouse

a poet who dwells among rational
houses sealed up like tombs. He listens
intently, his mind like his window ajar.
How faint her footsteps sound, and strange.

Encysted

Rising from the ground where my mountain bike
had thrown me, I dusted off and assessed
the damage: bruises blossoming on both legs,
a hand twice punctured by shrubby stalks.

My doctor cleaned and sutured the wounds.
One healed quickly, the other oozed pus
till it popped out half an inch of woody
stem. Months later, the doctor's scalpel
found another sliver enclosed in
a tiny capsule of tissue. *Encysted,*
he said, gripping the culprit with tweezers.

Thus I learned how the body disarms
what it can't fend off. Likewise, the mind?
Failure, regret, embarrassment, a fall
from grace or bike: can those irritants be
neatly excised from memory? I know
of no such procedure. So when they
fester, I encyst them in lines like these.

Mona Lisa Responds to Latest Assault

Paris, January 28, 2024

You ask whether the incident altered
my smile, reshaped it even briefly
to the *O* of horror in Munch's *The Scream*.
That might have happened were I as young
and naïve as the two *jeunes femmes* who splashed
my face with soup. But I've endured worse,
jostled in Leonardo's saddlebag
on our journey from Italy to Amboise;
kidnapped from the Louvre and kept two years;
attacked with acid, rock, razor blade,
cream cake, teacup. With each assault, oddly,
I've become more distant, more mysterious,
and, yes, more famous. I am Art, worshipped
alike in contemplation and the desperate
theatrics of those who crave attention
to themselves or their cause. Who remembers
them? Behind my shield of bulletproof glass,
I smiled as they took the vandals away.

Guy walks into a bar

and orders a beer, a shot of whiskey,
or a Bloody Mary. Sometimes he's
a woman, a horse, a duck, a panda,
or a termite. You've heard this story
before, or one just like it, but you
follow it down the familiar road,
watching for an unexpected turn.

Suppose the guy's a minister. He'll bring
a rabbi and a priest. Otherwise,
he'll have to talk to the bartender.
He'll order that drink. He'll ask a question
or be asked. That's how these stories work.

You listen carefully, all ears,
determined not to be the last to catch
the double meaning, to understand
the misunderstanding, to get the joke.
Who wants to seem as dumb as the guy,
or maybe this time it's the bartender?

You try to memorize the story, word
for word, so you can walk into a bar
and get it right. *Guy walks into a bar,*
you'll say, and everyone will pay attention.
They'll follow you down that road, happy
to be with a guy who knows the way.

23 and Me

Here is what the Seer told me, reading
the strands of my DNA like tea leaves:
You can probably smell asparagus
in your urine. *Check.* But you may not
be able to match musical pitch. *Check.*
Your genome is northwestern European
with a bit more Neanderthal than
average. Your paternal ancestry
includes Bourbon kings, your maternal
a woman buried as a Viking warrior.

She mentions no spiritual lineage,
leaving me to wonder how I'm related
to Zoroaster, Moses, Jesus, Muhammad,
the Buddha. They descended like me
from an Adam and Eve in East Africa,
though Jesus may be a special case.
As son of God, he claimed a chromosome
without precedent or recorded issue.

The Neanderthal in me wants to know
why those godly messengers showed up so
late. They swam in a film no thicker than
an oil slick on the deep well of human
history. Entire species like us
had gone extinct before they arrived.

The Seer bends closer to the tea leaves.
I see no future for your haplogroup,
she says, frowning at the damaged strands

and dead-end variants. But now you have
religion to ease your mortal passage,
not to mention the chocolate ice cream
that most in your group prefer to vanilla.

Living Room

First you notice what isn't there:
the couch, coffee table, TV,
and easy chair they took with them
when they moved. The people aren't

there either, nor their dog, nor
the toddler who giggled when
her bare feet brushed carpet. Then
you see what remains: footprints

of departed furniture, naked
curtain rods, dog-level smudges
on door frame, sun-jaundiced paint,
spectral shapes where pictures hung.

Others will move in tomorrow
or next week. They will fill the space
with things that tell them who they are.
Meanwhile the room, furnished simply

with silence and light, is taking
back its soul, rediscovering
which wall gives back the morning sun,
which corner keeps a piece of night.

Haunted

The house seemed too empty to be haunted—
no ghostly apparitions, no pipe organ
riffs at midnight. The gray clapboard siding
had forgotten paint or never knew it.

A developer planted houses in its
cornfields, then hired a crew to tear it down.
Now or never, my friend and I decided,
daring each other to enter first.

We found nothing inside to be afraid of.
The crew had crowbarred lath and plaster
from wall studs, spilling makeshift insulation
onto the floor, yellowing confetti

of letters and newspaper. We eavesdropped
on people gone long since to their graves,
small talk about the news and weather,
weddings and funerals, a crop just planted

or harvested, babies sick or thriving.
Had they found warmth in those letters,
read them one more time before interring
them in walls to stop the winter wind?

When the wrecking crew returned, we watched
them drop the house and haul it away, leaving
its ghosts with nowhere to stay except
with us, who were last to hear their stories.

Mushroom Hunters

They emerged from the fog
like monks cowled in floppy hats,
eyes downcast, walking slowly
as though in meditation.

Each carried in the crook
of one arm a basket to cradle
the ghostly fruit that erupted
from our vacant lot in fall.

They were trespassing,
my father said, yet he neither
fenced nor posted the field
I mowed each spring for baseball.

Thus did we concede their claim
to places they knew better
than we did, places older than
baseball, deeper than fences.

Couch Diving

My sister and I shouldn't have been
surprised when the map we'd sent away
for marked no place near us with an *X*
where pirates had buried gold doubloons.
We lived in Wisconsin. Why would pirates
haul their heavy chests so far inland?

Seeking another way to supplement
our allowance, we discovered treasure
in our living room couches. No picks
or shovels required, just hands small
enough to squeeze through narrow tunnels
into caves beneath the cushions.

Working blind, spelunking without headlamps,
our fingers sorted through popcorn kernels,
hair pins, and ticket stubs to the cold hard cash.
We kept the coins and gave away the rest—
pocket knives, cigarette lighters, and once
a funny balloon in a foil package.

It was boom and bust mining, no solution
to our cash flow problem, so my sister
babysat and I delivered papers.
We still dove the couches now and then,
after a party. But the thrill of finding
treasure faded as we grew older,
old enough to lose loose change to couches.

The Revenant

In dreams I sometimes haunt houses
I've lived in, passing from room to room
unseen by those I used to live with.
Tonight, it's the last home I shared
with parents and siblings, newly built
in a lasso loop of subdivision.

Entering by the back door, I find
my mother taking clothes from the dryer,
her first after years of pinning wash
to clotheslines. A farm girl now planted
in a field where corn once flourished,
she may be the least displaced of us.

Climbing stairs, I pass my sister's room.
Through her closed door I hear a radio
playing top 20 hits, counting backward
to the Beach Boys' *Surfin' USA*.
Down the hall, Dad bends over his desk,
preparing monthly expense reports
and chewing that place inside his cheek
Mom tells him to leave alone, let it heal.

My brother isn't in our room. I find
him outside, feeding our Lab retriever.
The dog's ruff goes up as I approach.
Has he forgotten our frosty mornings
in a duck blind? I want to tell my brother

it's true, what they say about dogs: they
can sense presences we humans can't.

But I'm voiceless in these dreams and must soon
reoccupy the body I left sleeping
many miles from here, many years from now.

The Green Trunk

What drew me to our dimly lit attic
as a boy was the olive drab metal trunk
containing my father's war—fatigues
that smelled mustily of West Africa,
medal ribbons and winged Army Air Corps
insignia, the corporal's stripes he wore
when he married my mother in '44.

Not until I returned from Vietnam
did I ask about his war, veteran
to veteran. Deflecting the personal,
he spoke of bombers he'd crewed, what mighty
workhorses they were. I noticed the tremor
in his hands, the way he turned his good ear
toward me to listen. So I took my cue
from him. I described the Cobra gunship
I'd seen working a tree line near Chu Lai.

My uniform hung in a back closet,
sheathed in plastic from the dry cleaner.
Years later, I stored the rest of my war
in the trunk I inherited from Dad.

My Grandfather's Kodak

When you unfold that folding Kodak
(number 3, model F), the lens and bellows
come at you like a locomotive emerging
from a tunnel. You wouldn't be surprised
to see steam gushing from the viewfinder
that sits like a smokestack above the lens.

Which is how it should be, Grandpa. You were
twenty-three when the camera was new
and you left home in Port Huron to ride
the rails as a machinist. By the time
I came along you were retired, a full-time
gardener. The Kodak's leather skin was scuffed,
your hearing dimmed by engine thunder.

Browsing your album after you died,
I found stiffly posed pictures of family,
but none from those years of bachelor
wandering. Hoping to resume where you
left off, maybe conjure any ghosts
that still lingered in the camera's dark
recesses, I took it to a photo shop
and asked the man for film to fit it.

He studied the string of patents stamped
inside, ending in 1902. When he
shook his head and gave it back, I knew
another part of you was past retrieving.

The Handoff

Watching two figures from a dorm window,
you might wonder what they were up to.
Lovers meeting under cover of darkness?
A junkie scoring drugs? That would explain
the package passed furtively between them.

As one of those figures, I can assure
you our meetings were neither passionate
nor illicit. In the small New England
college town where we started our family,
there was just one movie house. It made up
for its single screen with rapid turnover.
But if you missed *Annie Hall* or *Star Wars*
this week, you may have missed it altogether.

Hence our handoff, practiced till we were
a passable relay team. One babysat
at home, eyes on clock, while the other
caught the early show. When credits rolled,
we took a shortcut through campus to our
rendezvous. First sitter handed baby off
and hurried to make the second screening.

Come to think of it, we were lovers
after all—of each other, our child, and film.
Addicts, too, if you include those who crave
images of other lives, other times,
other places. Not to escape our
narrow circumstance, but to enlarge
and quicken our remarkable life.

Golden

for Puck, née Betty

Even in the city apartment
you saw the farm girl's practiced hand
as she unraveled an apple's skin

in a single looping strand from stem
to blossom end. When all were sliced
and bedded in a pie tin lined

with dough, she dangled a paring
before the boy and asked, *Want to know
whom you will marry?* He nodded yes,

as though at five he could conceive
a life besides the one they lived,
scented with cinnamon on baking days.

He cupped the green coil in both palms,
mounted a stool and tossed it over
his shoulder. Then they bent to read

the vatic scrawl. Was it a *B*
that half recalled the sphere it came from?
So his sibyl said, and so he still

believes, wedded fifty years to one
whose name the paring prophesied.
Now it's her turn to carve unbroken

spirals from apples. He chips them
into dough-lined tins. On baking days,
their kitchen smells of cinnamon.

Zoe Dances

Watching her spin across
the kitchen floor, arms extended
left and right for balance,
we wonder how we'd missed it:
our granddaughter is destined
to be a prima ballerina.

Last week, observing how
she tracked a column of red ants
up a sycamore, we were sure
she'd become a naturalist.

The week before, she was
another Julia Child,
stirring in her saucepan
an imaginary Béarnaise.

What did our grown-ups foresee
for us at fifteen months?
Bruised from bumping against
the ceiling of early promise,
they needed to believe
in our limitless potential.

We wear those bruises too,
so we draw no conclusions
when Zoe lands dizzy
and diaper-bottomed on the floor.

The Picture Above Our Bed

When did our sleek whitewater kayaks
become that wooden rowboat, calloused
with old paint like the one my grandparents
kept at their cottage? It floats on water
without a ripple, unlike the torrents
we paddled each spring. We wore wetsuits
and helmets, stowed our lunch in dry bags.

The couple in the painting are dressed
for a proper *déjeuner,* she in skirt
and blouse, he in white shirt and gallused
trousers. Broad-brimmed hats shade both faces.
Their picnic hamper no doubt contains
a tablecloth, long stem glasses, and bottle
of wine. How quaint they seemed when we hung
the picture forty years ago, never
suspecting we would become their peers.

We've come to admire their teamwork. He steadies
the boat with oars to port and starboard
as she leans over the transom, reaching
for a water lily. Will she ever pluck
that blossom? We hope not. Now that we've
caught up with them, we want him to keep
their craft upright, her to keep on reaching.

The Good Ship *Point Reyes*

Darwin had his *Beagle,* we have our *Point
Reyes,* docked at Olema, California,
on its voyage north. We share the trip
with more specimens than Darwin collected,
more animals than Noah squeezed into
his ark. Elk and dairy cows range freely
on deck, sparing our crew the drudgery
of forking out fodder and mucking out stalls.

The *Point Reyes* is a floating paradise
except for this: it rides a track like those
little boats in Disneyland that travel
a loop to choruses of *It's a Small World.*
Our piece of Pacific crust will grind
up the coast to Alaska, dive under
North America, and be melted down
to magma in Earth's interior furnace.

This would worry us if we expected
to reach Alaska. But we cruise by fits
and starts, our average speed less than
two inches per year. We're unlikely
to arrive, so we can afford to marvel
at the planet's recycling of resources—
old landforms continually giving birth
to new. It's a small world, after all.

Pact

So it's agreed, then: whichever of us
goes first into the unknown country will
return and tell the other what it's like.

We've always had each other to rely on,
remember passports and boarding passes,
decipher maps and signs in foreign languages.

Whoever's first will go disembodied
and alone into the next world, unschooled
in its customs and currency, its weather

and geography. The guidebooks give few
particulars. Is it true that people there
neither marry nor are given in marriage?

Do they wake to mornings like this one,
when fallen leaves are lightly furred with frost,
when the air is crisp as bitten apple?

If you go first and return as promised
to the room where we reveled in the warmth
of goose down on winter nights; if you stand

beside our bed as though struck dumb, wavering
between presence and absence, I will know
what you can't bring yourself to tell me.

My eyes, those two candles

light less each year. Will they
gutter out and leave me
in the dark? I don't know.

Yet their gradual dying
has this advantage: to see
something as though for

the last time is to see it
for the first time—tight
spirals of fern unfurling

in spring, for instance,
or neural networks of
lightning on summer nights.

In the firstness of final
sight the world lights up
like the face of one who,

grown used to being
overlooked, has at last
your undivided attention.

About the Author

Milton J. Bates earned a doctorate in English at the University of California, Berkeley and taught for thirty-five years, first at Williams College, then at Marquette University.

His scholarly books include *Wallace Stevens: A Mythology of Self* (University of California Press, 1985), editions of Stevens's uncollected writings and notebooks, and *The Wars We Took to Vietnam: Cultural Conflict and Storytelling* (University of California Press, 1996). He was appointed a Guggenheim Fellow (1989) and a Fulbright lecturer in China (2000) and Spain (2006).

Since retiring, he has published *The Bark River Chronicles: Stories from a Wisconsin Watershed* (Wisconsin Historical Society Press, 2012), the poetry collection *Stand Still in the Light* (Finishing Line Press, 2019), and two poetry chapbooks, *Always on Fire* (Five Oaks Press, 2016) and *As They Were* (YellowJacket Press), runner-up for the 2018 Peter Meinke Poetry Prize.

He lives with his wife in Michigan's Upper Peninsula, where they enjoy the region's year-round outdoor activities.

Made in the USA
Monee, IL
15 March 2025